ALL ABOUT MY SENSES

WHAT'S THAT SMELL?

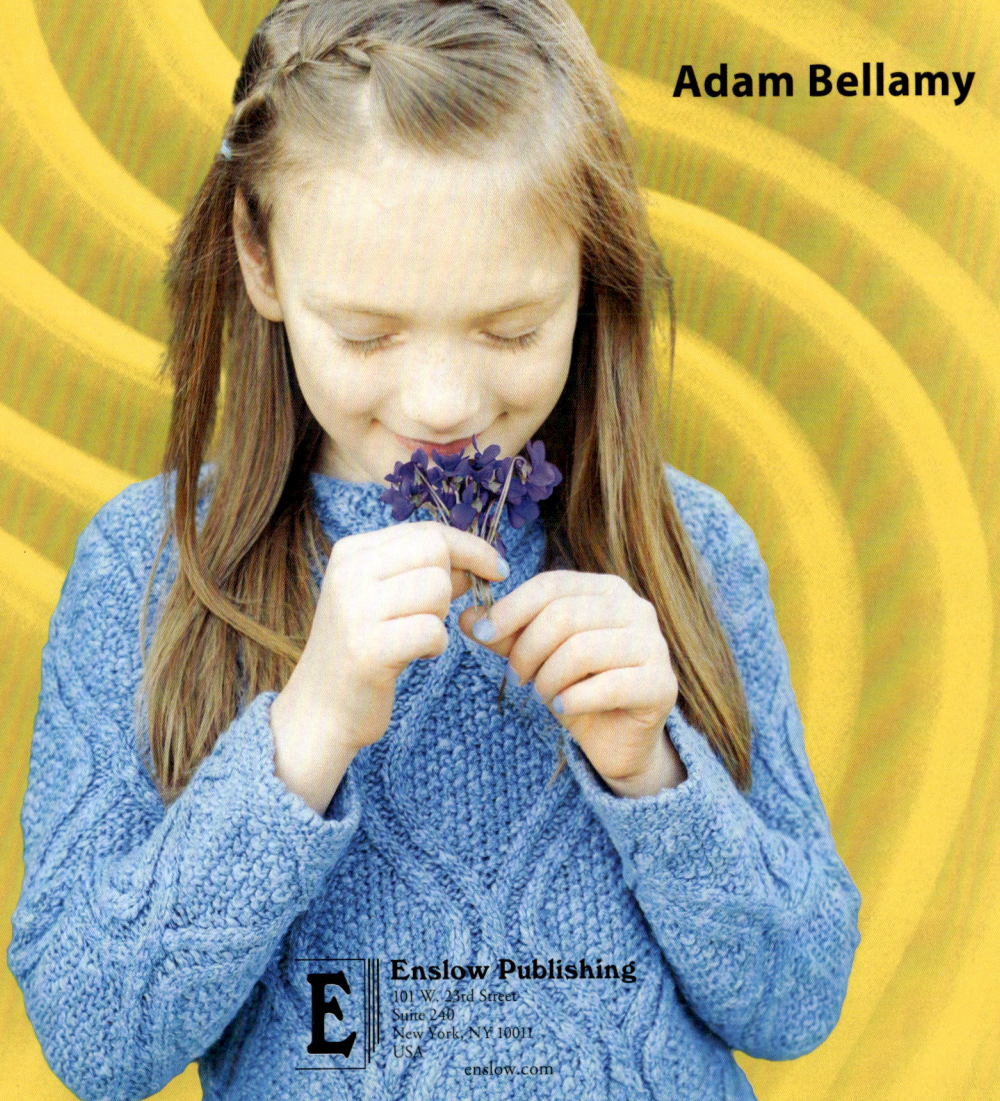

Adam Bellamy

Enslow Publishing
101 W. 23rd Street
Suite 240
New York, NY 10011
USA
enslow.com

Published in 2018 by Enslow Publishing, LLC.
101 W. 23rd Street, Suite 240, New York, NY 10011

Copyright © 2018 by Enslow Publishing, LLC.

All rights reserved.

No part of this book may be reproduced by any means without the written permission of the publisher.

Library of Congress Cataloging-in-Publication Data

Names: Bellamy, Adam, author.
Title: What's that smell? / Adam Bellamy.
Description: New York, NY : Enslow Publishing, 2018. | Series: All about my senses | Audience: Pre-K through grade 1. | Includes bibliographical references and index.
Identifiers: LCCN 2017002293| ISBN 9780766086074 (library-bound) | ISBN 9780766087934 (pbk.) | ISBN 9780766087941 (6-pack)
Subjects: LCSH: Smell—Juvenile literature. | Nose—Juvenile literature. | Senses and sensation—Juvenile literature.
Classification: LCC QP458 .B43 2018 | DDC 612.8/6—dc23
LC record available at https://lccn.loc.gov/2017002293

Printed in the United States of America

To Our Readers: We have done our best to make sure all websites in this book were active and appropriate when we went to press. However, the author and the publisher have no control over and assume no liability for the material available on those websites or on any websites they may link to. Any comments or suggestions can be sent by email to customerservice@enslow.com.

Photo Credits: Cover, p. 1 Anna Nahabed/Shutterstock.com (girl smelling flower), Flavio Edreira/EyeEm/Getty Images (background); lilam8/Shutterstock.com (spine graphic); pp. 3 (left), 10 Peter Gudella/Shutterstock.com; pp. 3 (center), 20 IgorAleks/Shutterstock.com; pp. 3 (right), 14, 22 Gelpi/Shutterstock.com; p. 4 GOLFX/Shutterstock.com; p. 6 mypokcik/Shutterstock.com; p. 8 Moving Moment/Shutterstock.com; p. 12 sestovic/E+/Getty Images; p. 16 Sheila Fitzgerald/Shutterstock.com; p. 18 Maria Uspenskaya/Shutterstock.com.

Contents

Words to Know 3

My Sense of Smell 5

Read More 24

Websites 24

Index 24

Words to Know

garbage    laundry 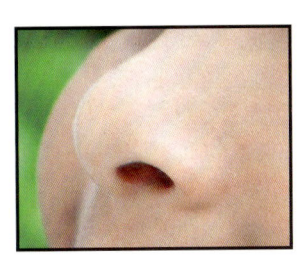   nose

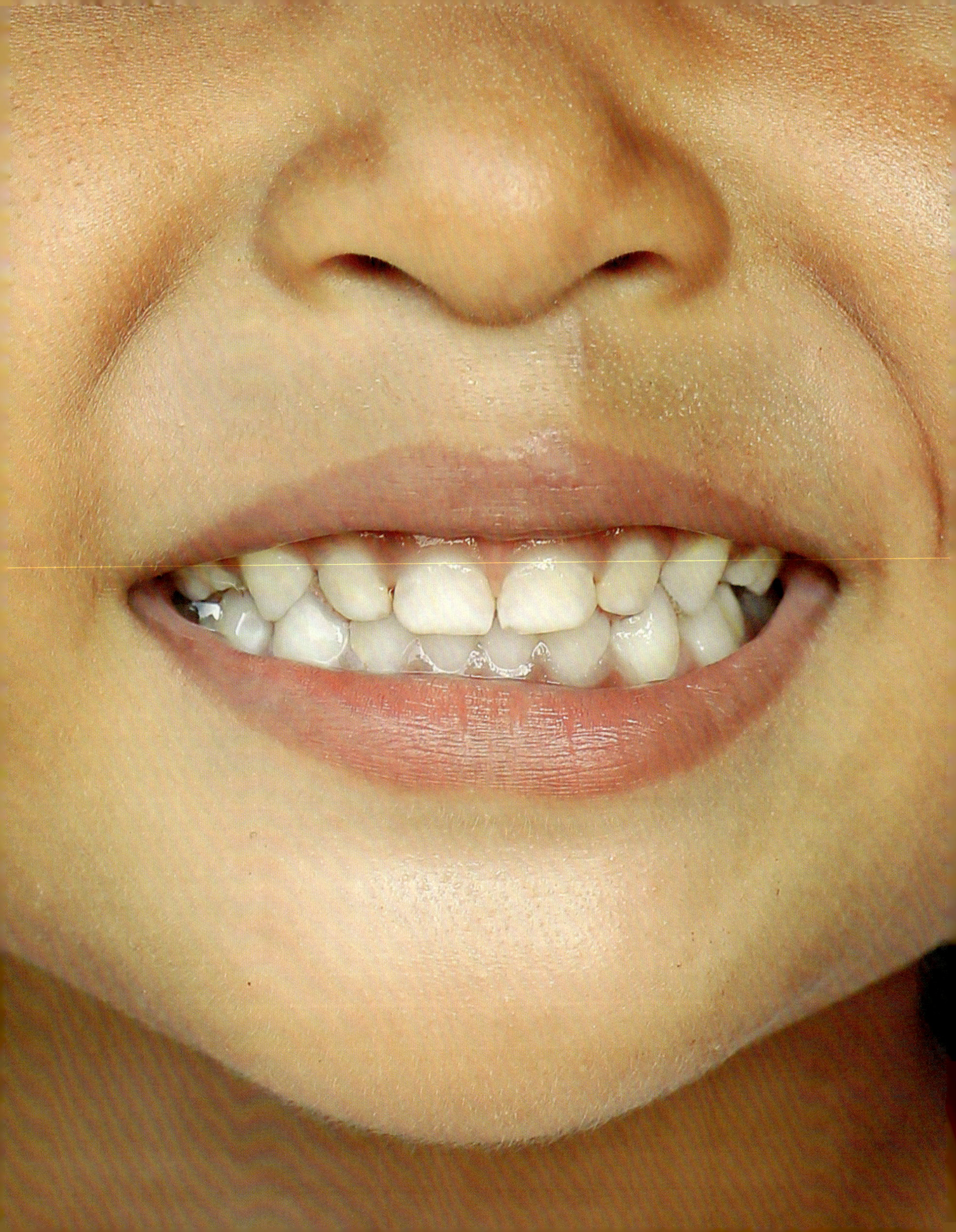

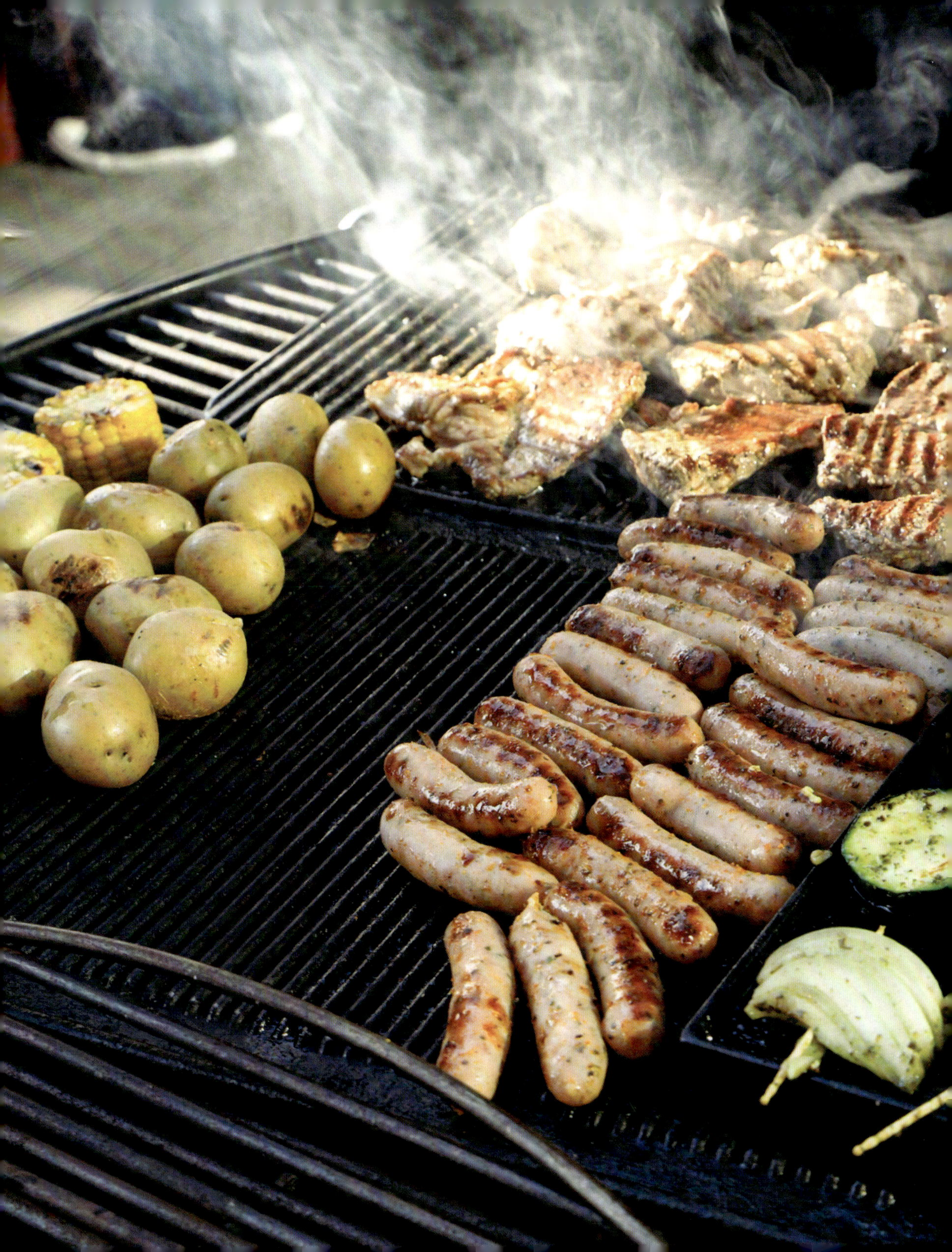

What do I smell when I sniff a flower? Flowers smell sweet.

My sense of smell is very important. I use my **nose** to smell. Some things smell good. Other things smell bad.

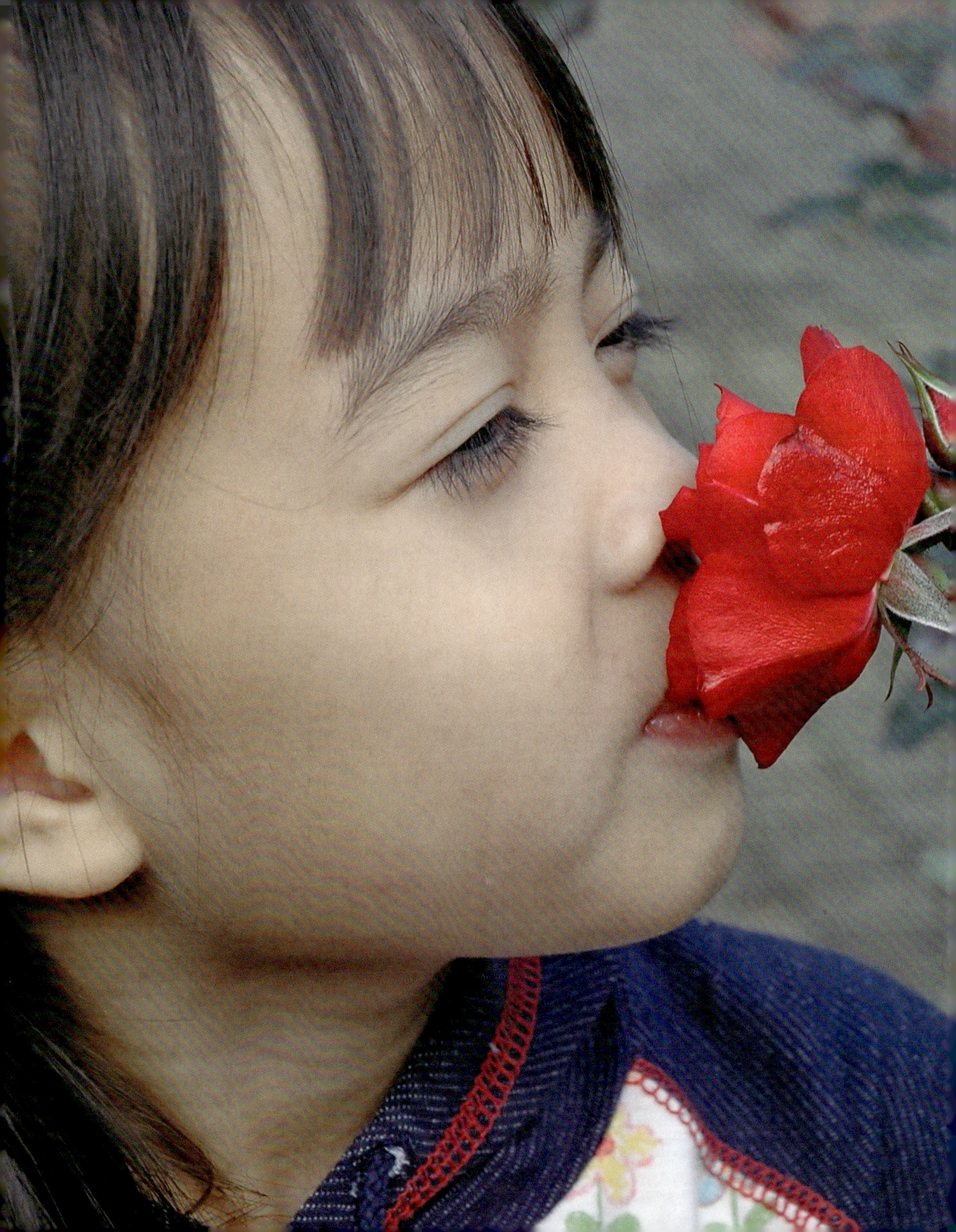

What's that delicious smell?
It's food cooking on a grill!
My sense of smell is stronger
when I'm hungry.

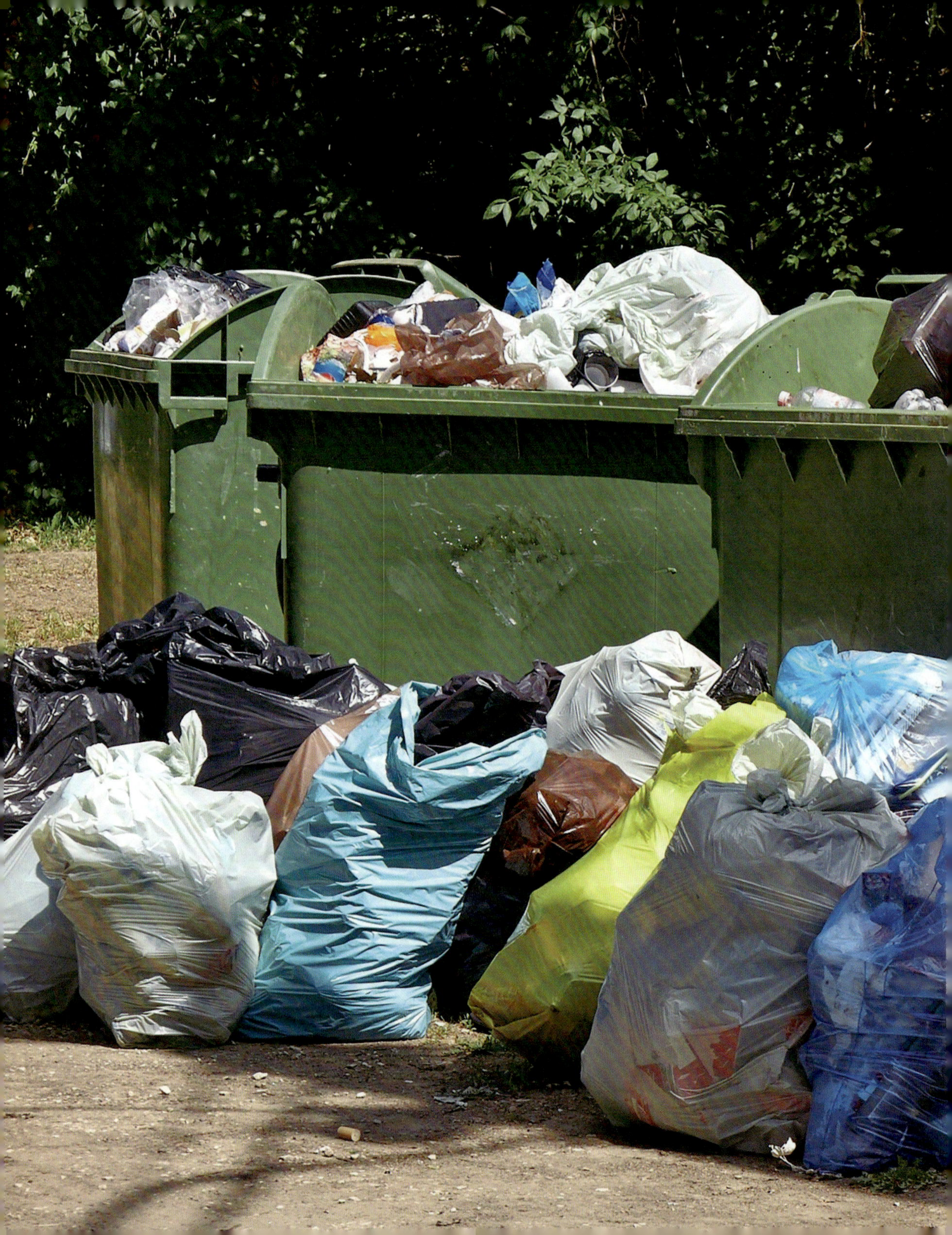

What's that bad smell?
That's stinky garbage.
Garbage smells worse in
hot weather.

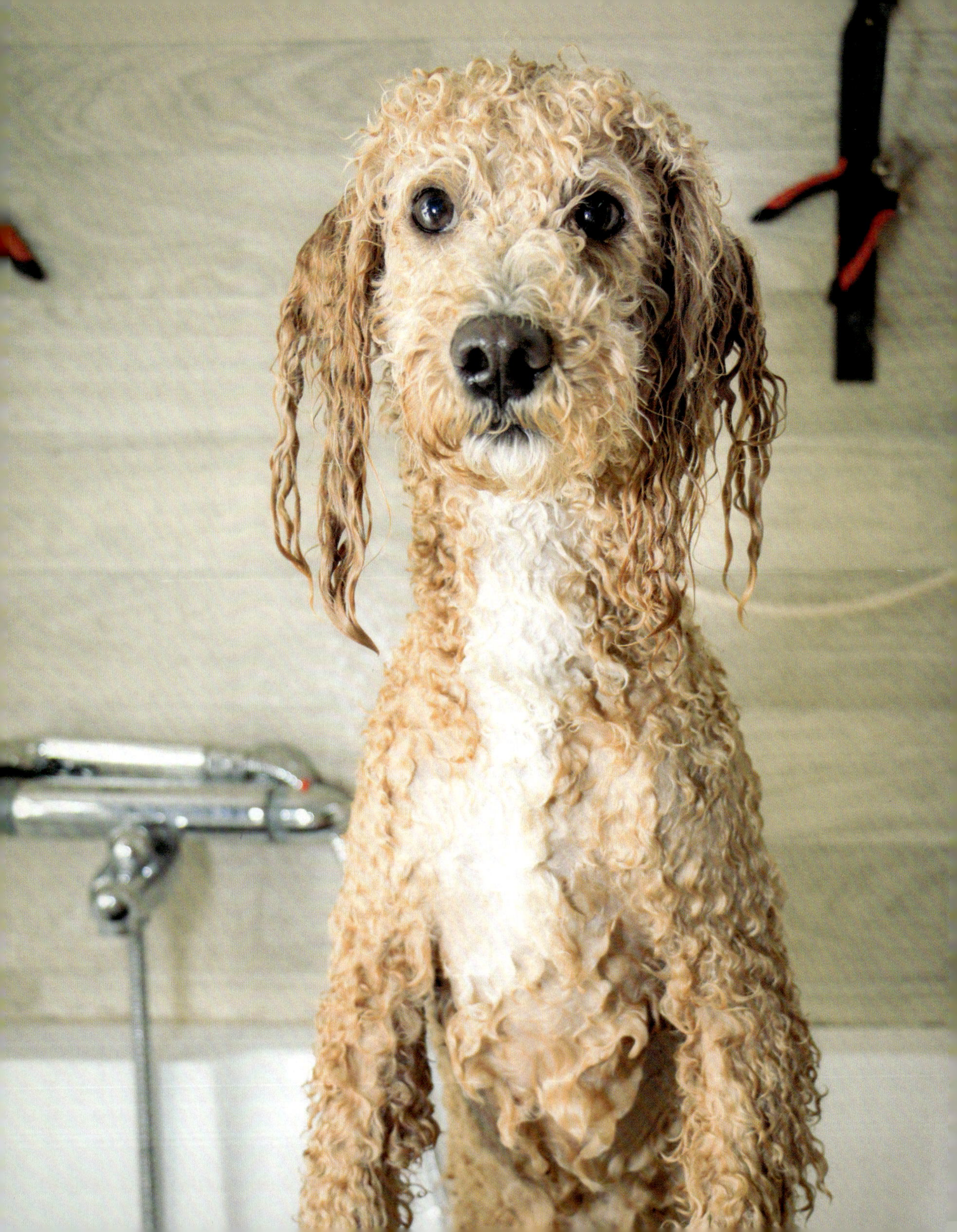

The dog smells bad when he's wet.

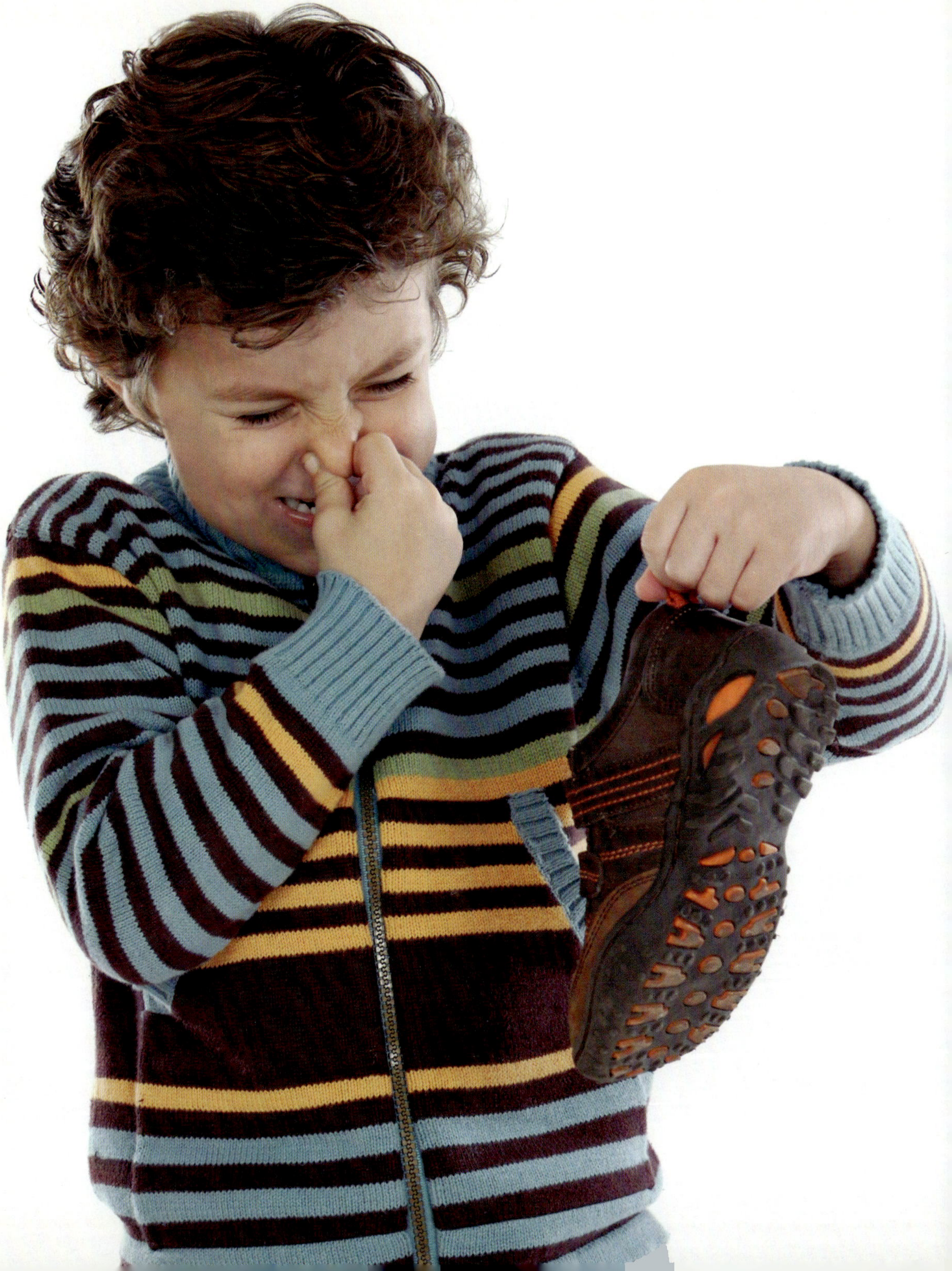

Shoes smell bad when they're worn out or dirty.

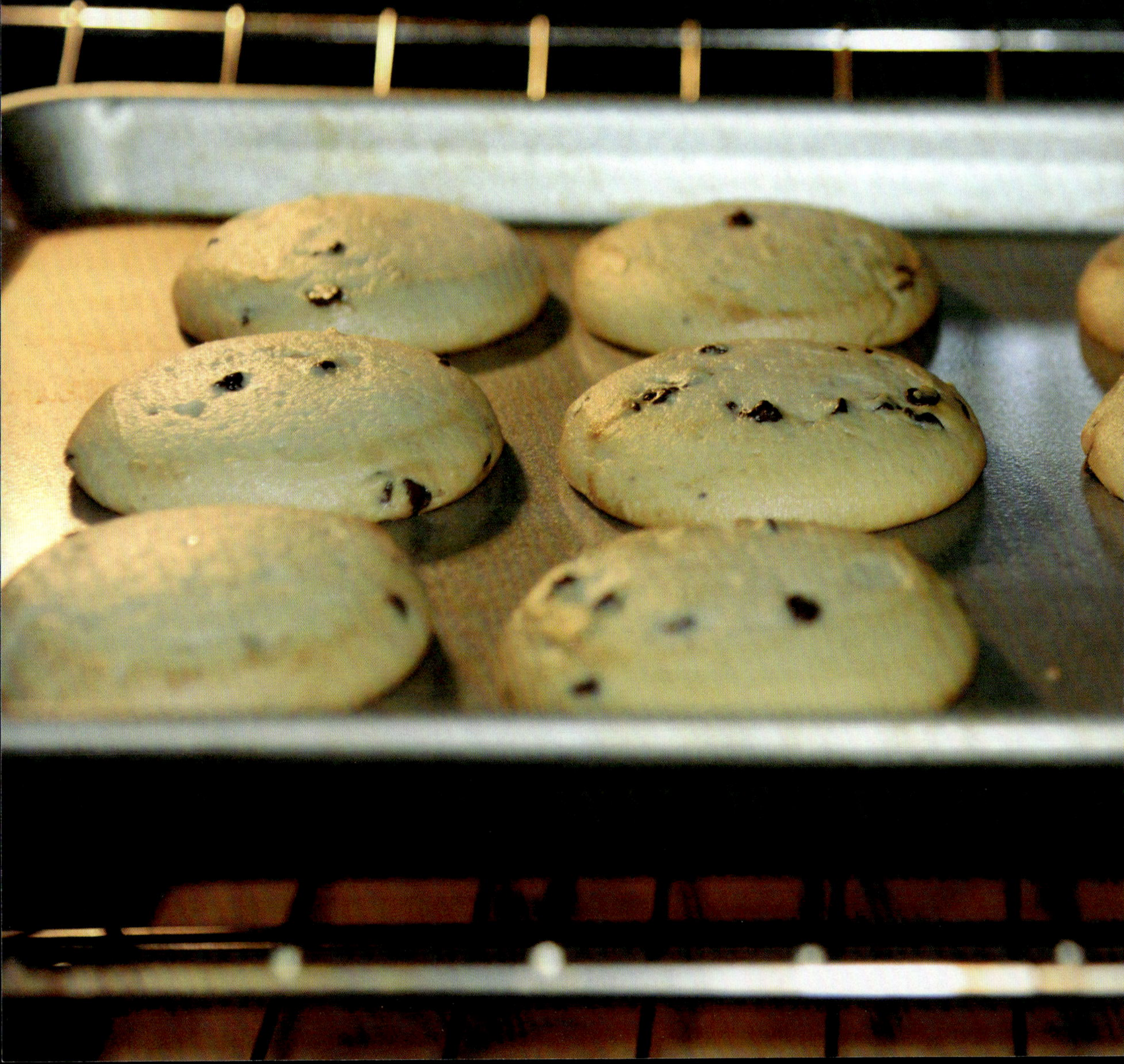

Cookies baking in the oven smell yummy.

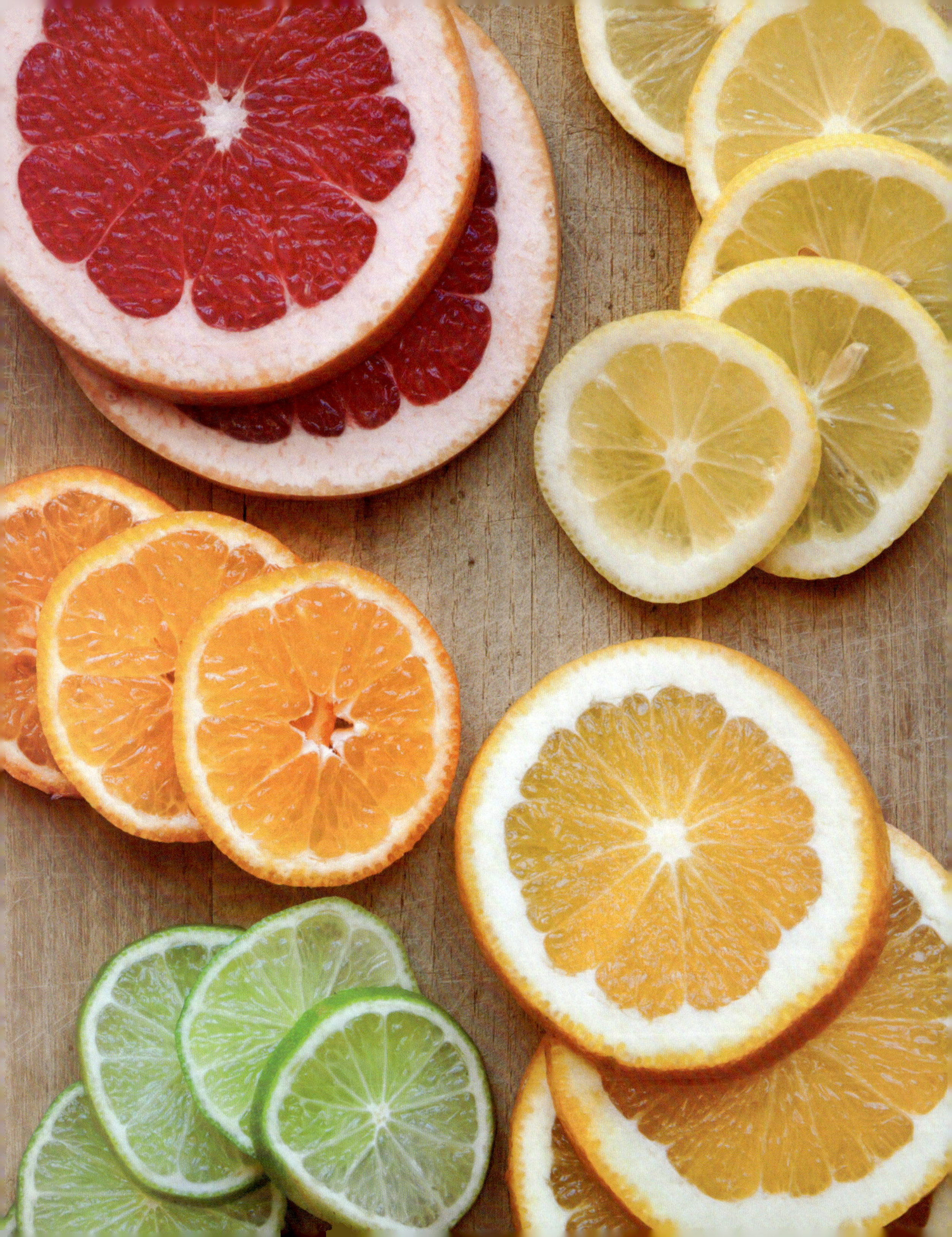

Oranges, lemons, and limes have a strong smell when you cut into them.

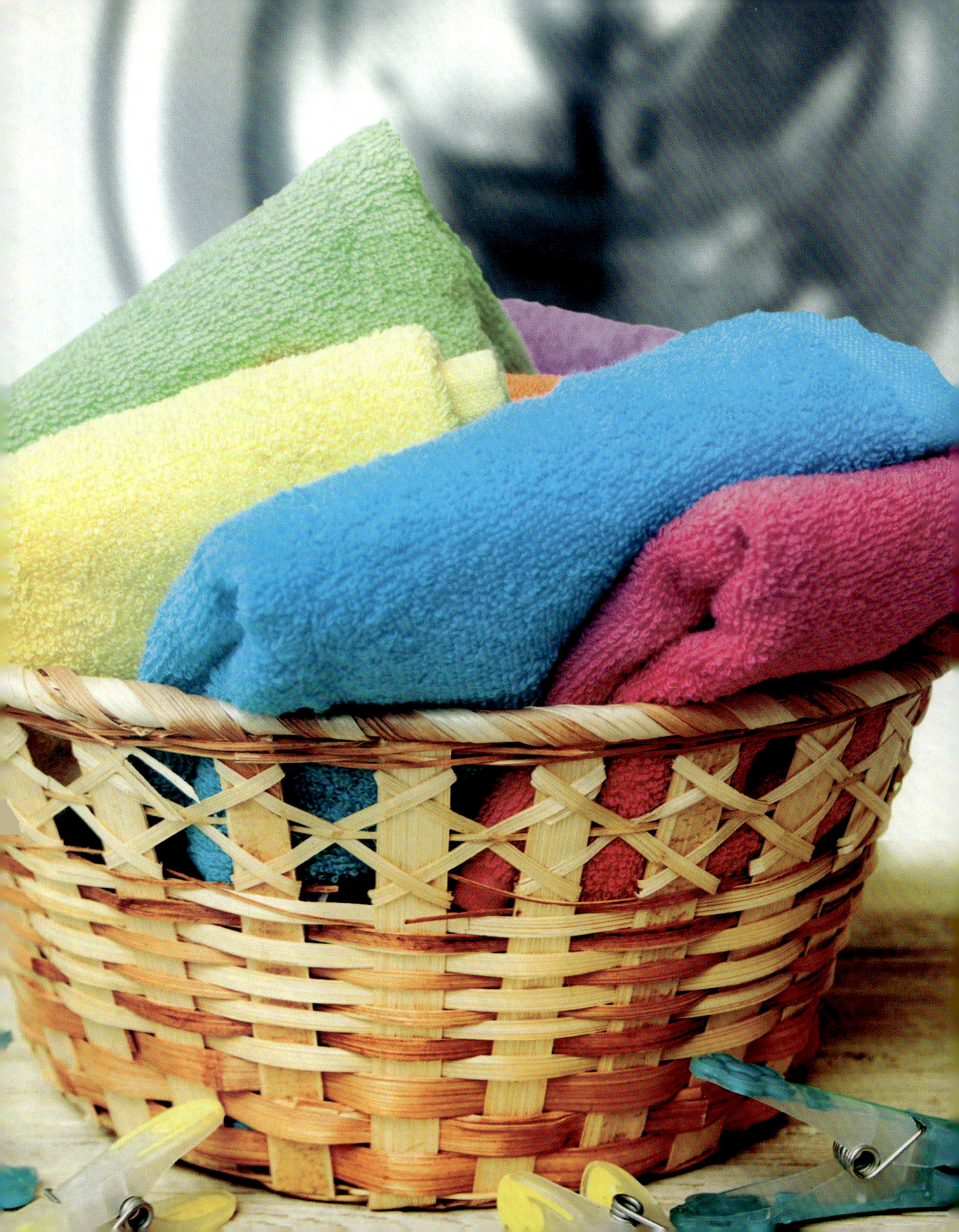

Clean laundry smells nice. It smells like the soap you use to wash the clothes.

I smell many different things every day.

Read More

Issa, Joanna. *What Can I Smell?* Portsmouth, NH: Heinemann, 2014.

Murray, Julie. *I Can Smell.* Minneapolis, MN: Abdo Kids, 2015.

Wheeler-Toppen, Jodi Lyn. *Our Noses Can Smell.* North Mankato, MN: Capstone Press, 2017.

Websites

ABCYa.com
www.abcya.com/five_senses.htm
Fun cartoons help you learn about your senses.

Science for Kids
www.scienceforkidsclub.com/senses.html
Learn more about the senses.

Index

cookies, 17
dog, 13
flowers, 7
garbage, 3, 11

hungry, 9
laundry, 3, 21
lemons, 19
limes, 19

nose, 3, 5
oranges, 19
shoes, 15
soap, 21

Guided Reading Level: C
Guided Reading Leveling System is based on the guidelines recommended by Fountas and Pinnell.

Word Count: 123